storage
solutions

Margaret Sabo Wills

BONNIER
BOOKS

BONNIER BOOKS

This edition published by Bonnier Books,
Appledram Barns, Birdham Road, Chichester,
West Sussex PO20 7 EQ, UK
www.bonnierbooks.co.uk

WELDON OWEN GROUP
Chief Executive Officer **John Owen**
Chief Financial Officer **Simon Fraser**

WELDON OWEN INC.
Chief Executive Officer and President **Terry Newell**
Senior VP, International Sales **Stuart Laurence**
VP, Sales and Marketing **Amy Kaneko**

VP, Creative Director **Gaye Allen**
Senior Art Director **Emma Boys**
Designers **Diana Heom** and **Anna Giladi**

VP, Publisher **Roger Shaw**
Executive Editor **Elizabeth Dougherty**
Managing Editor **Karen Templer**
Project Editor **Veronica Peterson**
Editorial Assistant **Sarah Gurman**

Production Director **Chris Hemesath**
Production Manager **Michelle Duggan**
Colour Manager **Teri Bell**

A WELDON OWEN PRODUCTION
Copyright © 2008 Weldon Owen Inc.

ISBN: 978-1-905825-55-4

10 9 8 7 6 5 4 3 2 1

Printed in China.

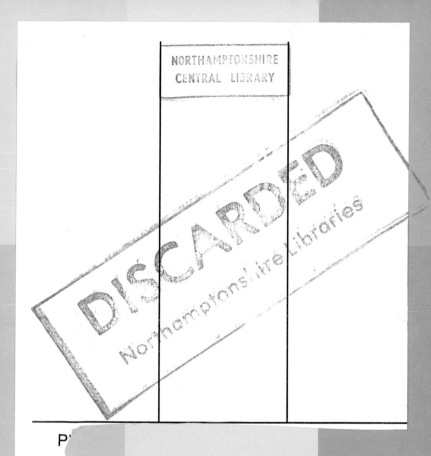

P'

contents

the organised life

Back in the overstuffed Victorian era, William Morris counselled, "Have nothing in your houses that you do not know to be useful, or believe to be beautiful." He said nothing about how best to store the belongings that meet that standard, but it remains a good guiding principle in our own time of abundance.

So what do we do with it all? Storage problems are the result of clutter—an excess of stuff. Storage solutions begin with separating the trash from the treasures. If you blanch at the idea of decluttering a whole house, take it one room (or even one drawer) at a time. Arm yourself with four containers—rubbish, recycle, give away and store—and then scrutinise each item. If you don't use it but someone else could, pass it along, but you might be surprised at how much you discard. As you go, remind yourself that gifts require a warm thank-you, not necessarily a lifelong home; that you needn't always keep an object to hang on to the memory it represents; and that, without all the clutter, prized possessions will have greater presence.

After the streamlining, assess what's left. The key to organisation is to group like things. In the kitchen, we put cutlery in one drawer, tea towels in another. Use this same approach throughout the house. When you've sorted out your belts, scarves and necklaces, or your brushes, paints and hand tools, you can start to see what sorts (and sizes) of shelves, cabinets or containers each group will require—and to think about which oft-used tools or favoured objects you'll want out in the open, and which you'd prefer to stow away.

Finding just the right place for every last thing will take some determination and a little creativity, but at this point you're already headed toward a more organised and efficient life. Let William Morris's words and this book be your guide.

living

There's no getting around it: life equals stuff. But when you strike the right balance between closed storage and artful display, that stuff is what gives a room life. Put your best belongings on open shelves and stow more mundane things in drawers or behind doors.

geared for daily life

It takes only one individual to create a storage calamity, but the more people there are in a given household, the greater the challenge of keeping your living space tidy.

shelve it

Shelving is an essential item, but it can be as simple as boards on milk crates or as elaborate as custom built-ins. Explore the wide range of styles now available for every budget and plan to use your shelves for far more than just books.

multi-task

Choose furniture that earns its floor space by doubling as storage: a coffee table with drawers; a lidded ottoman; a room divider of open shelving; or a wall unit configured for books, a television, a stereo, and all of the corresponding media.

seek trouble

Note which spots are magnets for household flotsam and address them accordingly. If newly arrived magazines get strewn all over the house, appoint a shelf for them. If shoes pile up by a couch, place a sturdy basket nearby.

give cues

Keep things categorised and in logical places, and don't be shy about labels and dictums. The more clearly you are able to convey where every last thing goes, the more likely the whole family will be to stick with whatever system you've created.

contain it

Storage supply shops sell boxes and bins for every conceivable purpose, in a wide range of styles, but you'll also want to scout out idiosyncratic options. Look for old shoe racks, blanket chests or retail display cases for instance.

go vertical

Maximise storage with furniture that uses height for extra capacity, such as a wall-mounted shelf or cabinet in an otherwise unused spot. Activate the space above doors by running a single shelf around a whole room, just below the ceiling.

the family library

Books are at their very tidiest—and thus better companions for a mix of objects—when lined up along their spines. Book stands display treasured volumes.

mixed media Since DVDs, CDs, tapes and records come in uniform sizes, they slip neatly into shelves of corresponding heights, either with or without doors.

made for tv

Media cabinetry can be designed to hide the television or to highlight it. In either case, keep remotes under control by designating a caddy.

framing device Just as matching frames can unify an assortment of pictures, bookcases can tie together disparate contents—whether extra pillows or a television.

the best storage is that which leaves room for character

Books have a way of mounting up, which is part of their charm for many readers. These gleaming metal shelves provide a framework for a collection but without forcing it into regimented rows. The shelves are deep enough to accommodate oversize art volumes or doubled stacks of smaller books.

let the sun shine in

Allowing space for generous
windows, a harmonious band
of low shelving holds books
and magazines, continuing as
drawers under a window seat.
Matching shelves across the
room support a large mirror.

in plain sight In a hallway (above), floor-to-ceiling ledges face art books forward. Artworks on wide mouldings (right) allow new acquisitions to be seen.

woodpile redux

For uninterrupted
fireside evenings,
store logs nearby—in
a framed-out niche,
stacked tidily under
the hearth ledge or
in a sturdy tub or pot.

go wide A low, rough-planked cabinet spans this room, serving as both display ledge and catchall, while blending into the equally rugged timber frame interior.

setting boundaries See-through metal toy shelves delineate a play corner in this sleek living room. Similar chrome shelving does heavier duty in both spaces.

workspace

Whether you're working, spending time online or enjoying a favourite hobby, configuring a dedicated space for your chosen pursuit makes it easier to get down to business. The key to a workspace you'll love: storage specifically tailored to your task.

equipped for the job

The greatest benefit of having a tailored workspace
is the luxury of focus—you won't be constantly breaking
your concentration to hunt down what you need.

be particular

Ensure that your personal
workspace needs are
addressed by first sorting
out what they are. Is your
challenge to control craft
supplies, keep tools on
view, store big artworks
or manage paperwork?
List your concerns and
find a solution for each.

prioritise

Make the worktable or
desk your command
centre: keep your most
frequently used items
within reach and keep
everything else out of the
way. Archives, records
and anything rarely
accessed might go into
another space entirely.

make space

Desks, shelving, filing
cabinets and dividers
can define an office
within any open area,
giving it both privacy and
credence. Built-in desks
and shelving maximise
the space; freestanding
pieces offer flexibility as
your space needs evolve.

think small

Whether buttons and
threads, tubes of paint or
discs and manuals, small
things can be vital to your
work. Arrange like things
into groups and store
them in appropriately
sized containers, divided
drawers, slotted shelves
or labelled file folders.

know your style

If you crave a calm and
austere workspace, you'll
need ample drawers and
cabinets. If, on the other
hand, you feel inspired
when surrounded by
meaningful piles of stuff,
go for bulletin boards,
open shelves and lots of
available worktop space.

store safely

Will you be sharing office
space with a toddler or
a pet? If so, conceal
electrical wires in plastic
casing and stow away
any hazardous materials
and tools. Anchor top-
heavy bookcases and be
careful not to overload
any wall-hung shelves.

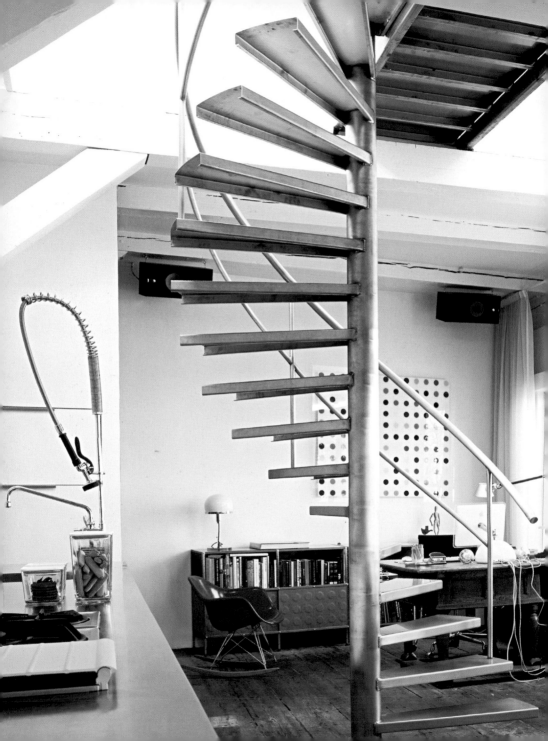

new definition At one end of an open loft, vintage sideboards and an antique desk conjure up a fully formed office, with a mix of open and closed storage.

labelled for use

Buckets labelled with colourful copies of their contents, supplies in clear boxes and cleverly marked file drawers make it easy to locate items.

work styles

Shelves and cabinets hung on
wall-mounted brackets (left)
form a hard-working backdrop
for a bright, streamlined desk.
Quieter neutrals (above) allow
a household command centre
to blend into the kitchen.

found space Offices can fit gracefully into unused nooks—in an under-stair alcove or on a landing. Shelving and matched boxes keep clutter under control.

behind closed doors With a laptop and ample vertical storage, even a cupboard can hold a compact office. And doors hide it away quickly and easily.

neutral space

A simple board on brackets
and a patch of hessian form
a quiet office in a bedroom
corner. Clipboards, a modified
clothesline and stacks of cigar
boxes bring order to the mix
of things on and over the desk.

eau de Jau

2

DE PENE FRANCE

NO. 700

Minter's *Deluxe*
CHOCOLATE DROPS

NET WT. 14 LBS.

Dark
Milk

MINTER BROTHERS, INC.
BRIDGEPORT, PA.

FORKS

KNIVES

1

CHATEAU
FOMBRAUGE

SAINT-EMILION GRAND CRU

2000   12x75 cl ℮

GRADE SCHOOL

PHOTOS

LETTERS

GUIDES

PHOTOS

LETTERS

10

under the eaves

To make room for a
desk, the contents of
this attic were boxed
up and inventoried.
Blueprint drawers
provide flat storage,
as does the factory
table turned worktop.

4

5

ready for work

Storage-rich tables, a wall
of tools, large cabinets and
a built-in desk add up to a
multipurpose workroom.

milo Ella ni

room to create

The focus of this family-friendly room is the work table—its shelves, drawers and bins brimming with the stuff of art. In/out baskets for the kids keep things in order. At the desk (left), an elevated Perspex surface keeps tools on view and at hand.

sew inspired

Clear jars and labelled
boxes organise scraps,
buttons and thread.
Ribbon spools are
threaded on a rod,
handy for sewing and
gift wrapping alike.

skein scheme Lucky for avid practitioners of the fibre arts, the requisite yarns and needles store beautifully out in the open, adding up to a richly textured display.

kitchens

Nowhere in the home are storage concerns more intensive than in the kitchen, where standard banks of cabinets are only the start. To make sure there is truly a place for everything—from spoons to spices, teacups to towels—you'll need to think outside the built-in box.

configured for cooks

No matter the size or style of your kitchen, getting it in order and keeping it that way hinges on everyone who uses the space knowing exactly what goes where.

be motion-minded

Observe how you use your kitchen to pinpoint organisational needs. Do you find you have to cross the room multiple times to accomplish any given task? If so, try to consolidate things used together near the point at which they're used.

think logically

Follow the golden rule of kitchen storage: place things near the fixture or appliance they relate to. Glasses should be next to the fridge, dish towels near the sink, pots and pans by the cooker. Keep extra rubbish bags in the bottom of the bin.

ask for proof

Reserve the most easily accessed areas—the worktops and those cabinets between waist and eye level—for the things you use most. Relegate holiday platters and other rarely used pieces to harder-to-reach spots, either high or low.

max out cabinets

With shelves too deep or too far apart, much of a cabinet's capacity can be wasted. Bring every inch into service with stacking risers, slide-out bins on rails, vertical dividers and lazy Susans. Wherever possible, attach racks and hooks to doors.

use displays

The stuff of hospitality— from condiment bottles and serving platters to table linens and fine china—humanises the atmosphere of a working kitchen. Consider storing these in the open, but be sure to keep them away from smoke and grease.

catch strays

Many kitchen storage challenges have nothing to do with the culinary arts. Set up permanent spots or even temporary holding zones for books, school bags, papers, toys and anything else that tends to collect on the kitchen table or worktops.

everything at hand Rails with S-hooks make a pan rack that much handier. Over an island, a suspended shelf keeps oils, preserves and seasonings in reach.

daily display

Behind an oft-used
range (left), oils line up
on a ledge over utensil
rails. Tea towels and
pot vegetables are
stashed in large bowls
beneath the island.
When kept on display,
collections of practical
items (above and
right) can be both
used and admired.

hidden assets

Running floor to ceiling and wall to wall, these smooth laminate cabinets offer an enviable amount of storage. Strategically placed niches break up the expanse and showcase collectibles.

rough ideas

Fruit crates tucked into doorless base cabinets increase this kitchen's utility—and its rustic appeal.

a stealth kitchen A silver tea service, glassware and brown pottery form quiet displays above base cabinets so elegant in design that they appear to be furniture.

attractive opposites A ceiling-height dresser demarcates an open kitchen. The wooden furniture stands in charming contrast to the stainless-steel cabinets.

a new view

In this 100-year-old brick building, once the town library, shelves now hold dining-room necessities, with vertical slots housing platters, cutting boards, rolled linens and wines.

objects of attention This kitchen's compact core, with tiny upper cabinets, gives a clean backdrop for shelves of colourful collectibles at the front of the space.

78

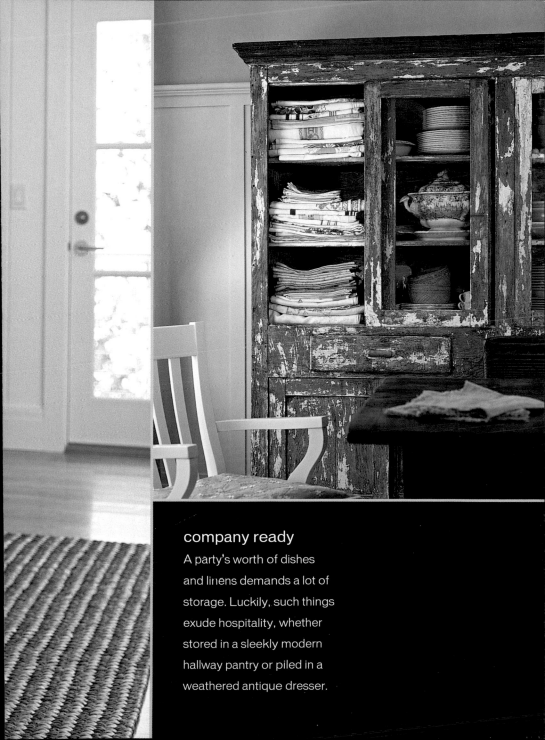

company ready

A party's worth of dishes
and linens demands a lot of
storage. Luckily, such things
exude hospitality, whether
stored in a sleekly modern
hallway pantry or piled in a
weathered antique dresser.

a decor dictum

Nearly everything is beautiful in multiples, here demonstrated by simple spice tins (left) and oils and vinegars massed in an antique tool-box (above). On "floating" shelves (right), groups of tin cups, canisters and coffee presses mingle with nature prints.

store and protect

Stow wine on its side not just for good looks and space savings, but to keep the corks from drying out. To prolong the wine's life, keep temperatures steady.

bathrooms

Though they're traditionally among the smallest rooms in a house, bathrooms can make big storage demands. Use space-smart strategies to gather all the toiletries, bath towels, medicines and cosmetics, and you'll soon be beginning (and ending) your day in organised bliss.

prepared for action

Bathroom storage often must accommodate multiple people and a high potential for clutter—frequently during the most hectic times of the day.

see the needs

Consider the role of the space. A guest bathroom, for example, might need to hold only extra toilet paper and hand towels, while a family bathroom must handle multiple family members and their towels and toiletries on a day-in, day-out basis.

conquer clutter

Scout out eye-catching containers to organise necessary gear, both on worktops and in the depths of the vanity unit. Trays or bins of related items not only keep things orderly but can also be pulled out as needed, then restowed.

ward off water

Bathroom furnishings and any open displays must contend with the splashing of water and general dampness that are characteristic of the space. Store dry towels where they'll stay fresh, and put bath toys where they can fully dry out.

think safety

Given a bathroom's often tight dimensions and wet surfaces, take steps to ensure that everyone can grasp what they need without any precarious reaching or climbing. And always store and use hair-driers and curling tongs away from water.

waste no space

Take full advantage of vertical space with hooks high on walls and on the backs of doors, and with shelving or a cabinet over the toilet. Store items used less often in higher spots and, for reaching them safely, provide a slip-resistant step stool.

rethink built-ins

A freestanding chest or bureau can be a stylish addition to a bathroom's built-ins while adding storage capacity. Sinks can be mounted in or on many types of furniture, so consider replacing a drab basin with a vintage chest, cabinet or table.

custom built

Built-ins abound in this spacious his-and-hers bathroom, where a bathside vanity table leads to a dressing alcove with a lidded storage bench.

warming trends

Wall-hung drawers (above) and doors of richly figured wood (right) conceal storage space in these contemporary bathrooms. The absence of shiny knobs downplays the furniture's utilitarian nature.

furnished for function Freestanding furniture adds style and storage capacity to any bathroom, but especially those lacking built-in vanity units or cabinets.

the little things

No need to hide the
cotton buds and
flannels—remove
necessities from their
packaging and group
everything in cups,
trolleys, jars or trays.

geometric proof Geometry conveys order, as demonstrated by the neat grids of built-in niches (left) and of stacked boxes punctuated by toilet-paper circles.

towel off

Sleek vanity units (left) substitute towel bars for drawers. A weathered towel rack (above) lends age and texture to a room. Folded and stacked in a glass-fronted cabinet (right), bath towels are integral to the room's maritime colour scheme.

wardrobes

Wardrobes can be a curse to anyone who tends toward messiness: it's too easy to slip up knowing the door will provide cover. But even if you're the only one who'll ever see it, a well-sorted and organised wardrobe is a thing of such beauty you'll be loath to mess it up.

maximised for capacity

Get the infrastructure of your cupboard right—whether it's designed to hold clothing or linens—and you'll find it easy to organise the contents and maintain order.

create more room

Increase the capacity of an insufficient wardrobe by reconfiguring it or adding shelves, drawers and rails. Hang shirts and trousers on tiered rails, installing the lower rail about 1 metre from the floor and the upper about 75 cm above that.

think extras

Inventory the non-clothes aspects of your wardrobe and work out the storage you'll need for jewellery, scarves, belts, ties and shoes. Boxes hold out-of-season clothing, while hooks on doors receive jackets, pyjamas or tomorrow's outfit.

light it up

Make the darker parts of a wardrobe more visibly accessible by having a simple light installed. If an electrician is beyond your budget, look for stick-on battery-powered lights. Glossy white paint on the interior walls will make everything easier to see.

invent space

If you need more room for clothes storage, you can frame in an extra cupboard or enclose an alcove with folding doors. A less labour-intensive option would be to mount racks and rails in a corner and use a curtain or floor screen for cover.

shop for help

Take a look at built-in wardrobes, or visit any home-improvement or organisational shop for modular prefabricated systems in laminate, fine wood or coated wire. You can use either approach to create a wardrobe or add to an existing one.

be generous

In hanging clothes, leave room for air to circulate, and allow enough space on the rails to remove an item without dislodging its neighbours. Give at least 5 to 10 cm from one shirt hanger to the next, and 10 cm between skirt and trouser hangers.

personal space A low chest of drawers and a simple wall of built-in clothes storage turn an awkward space under a roofline into a charming dressing room.

Island of calm

More luxurious than
a walk-in wardrobe is a
walk-around dressing
room, where rails and
drawers are just the
beginning. Trays in
various sizes, lined
up on shelves, keep
accessories sorted.
Out-of-season items
are safely stowed in
lidded, labelled boxes

newly configured

A standard wardrobe feels as capacious as a walk-in one when it's fully partitioned into easy-to-scan compartments.

sorting it out Whether in a glass-doored walk-in or a pullout trolley, the key to high-functioning clothes storage is to sort everything by colour, size and type.

clever disguise

Folding doors enclose an alcove to create a wardrobe. Coats slip discreetly behind a false wall. Papered to match, both cupboards blend into the walls.

smart steps Put the space beneath stairs to work with shoes slipped onto shelves behind the risers (above) or with pull-out sections in graduated sizes (right).

116

let's get dressed

A rail and curtains in front of built-in shelves and drawers create a spacious wardrobe (left). Graphic icons help kids sort their own clothes and shoes.

beyond the built-in A tent of creamy fabric and a curtain tie-back turn a
corner into a wardrobe; a row of peak-roofed cupboards evokes seaside huts.

second life

A deep picture frame acts as a shadow box for a family photo and heirloom jewels (left). Petri dishes and an antique cigarette tin (above and right) make surprisingly smart jewellery storage, separating chains and delicate pieces.

linen press reinvented

A trolley on casters (above) keeps stacks of folded sheets handy beneath a platform bed. An antique iron crib frame (right) displays a colourful collection of rolled quilts.

utility rooms

Wet weather gear, laundry supplies, sports equipment, garden tools–crucial but not glamorous elements of any household. To store these things and keep them accessible is the challenge of a utility room. Get it right and your household will run more smoothly than ever.

designed for use

Laundry rooms, boot rooms, utility spaces and supply cupboards are all meant to be behind-the-scenes aids in keeping a household running smoothly.

ease routines

In your mind or in reality, take a walk through the daily comings and goings of your family. Then plan suitable spots near doors or within hallways for everything you encounter along the way—from car keys and umbrellas to footballs and knapsacks.

get hooked

If your home doesn't have a boot room, mount a row of hooks along a wall near the main door, add a bench if space permits and line shoes up below. This will keep things tidy and accessible and provide a space for wet items to dry.

gather forces

Housekeeping tasks are inherently foreseeable and repetitive, which makes it a relatively easy exercise to collect all the tools and supplies for a given task into a handy location. There they will be reliably waiting to be called into service.

grab and go

Often, a utility room is used to stage supplies and tools to be used in other parts of the house. For maximum efficiency, line a shelf or cabinet with containers equipped for basic cleaning chores, small repair work and garden maintenance.

iron it out

If you prefer ironing in the living room or kitchen rather than the utility room, organise a nearby cupboard to take the ironing board and other necessities, rather than storing them in the utility room and hauling them back and forth.

borrow space

Garages often contain wasted space. Create a potting room at one end with a standard base cupboard and overhead shelves, or install ample cupboards and turn the entire garage into a mixed-use workshop the whole family can enjoy.

a proper greeting

Below hooks for hats and coats, a generous sideboard, baskets, boot cubbyholes and a pair of umbrella stands meet whatever comes through the front door.

mudless boot room Hooks and racks gather everything from brooms to boots. Wall-mounted cubbyholes, lined with mats, make room for a built-in dog bed.

all in the family

In a family cloakroom,
personalised cupboards,
assorted bins and a rack for
book bags coordinate today's
comings and tomorrow's
goings. Blackboards turn the
space into a message centre.

new laundry outlook

This spacious laundry room boasts folding space, a rolling laundry bin and overhead shelves. Sprays and soaps stored in pretty bottles and canisters make the job feel less like a chore.

a supply surprise Bright floral prints add whimsy to a household supply cupboard equipped with lined wicker baskets and convenient fabric holdalls.

pegged a winner Simple-to-install Peg-Board is as useful for toys as tools. Baskets of additional equipment are easily transported to the garden or park.

fertile ideas

Rows of deep drawers and
wide shelves—lined with trays,
canisters and bins—keep this
potting shed organised.

photo credits: **front cover** Narratives/Jan Baldwin/stylist Lesley Dilcock; **2** Hotze Eisma; **12** Narratives/Jan Baldwin/stylist Lesley Dilcock; **16** Camera Press, London/*Marie Claire Maison;* **17** Red Cover/James Balston; **19** Andreas von Einsiedel; **22-23** Narratives/Jan Baldwin; **26** Alexander van Berge/*Eigen Huis & Interieur*; **29-31** Hotze Eisma; **32-33** Eric Roth; **38-39** Hotze Eisma; **42** Mark Lund; **44** Red Cover/Alun Callender; **45** Red Cover/Paul Massey; **46** Eric Cahan; **47** Photozest /Inside/House of Pictures/L Wendendahl; **58** EWAStock.com/Andreas von Einsiedel; **59** Andreas von Einsiedel; **64** Red Cover/Niall McDiarmid; **65** Red Cover/Johnny Bouchier; **68-69** Hotze Eisma; **70-71** IPC Syndication/*Living Etc.*/Jake Fitzjones; **72-73** Lisa Romerein; **74-75** Hotze Eisma; **78-79** Lisa Romerein; **83** Hotze Eisma; **85 (top)** IPC Syndication/ *Living Etc.*/Winifried Heinze; **87** IPC Syndication/*Homes & Gardens*/Edina van der Wyck; **92** Red Cover/Warren Smith; **93** Fab-pics/Thomas Ott; **95** IPC Syndication/*Ideal Home*/Spike Powell; **96 (top)** IPC Syndication/*Living Etc.*/Craig Knowles; **98** Andreas von Einsiedel; **99** Camera Press, London/*Marie Claire Maison;* **100 (left)** Getty Images; **103** Camera Press, London/*Marie Claire Maison;* **106** Simon Kenny; **110-111** California Closet Company, Inc.; **112** Hotze Eisma; **113** Red Cover/ Chris Tubbs; **114-115** Camera Press, London; **116** IPC Syndication/*Living Etc.*/Jason Loucas; **117** Elizabeth Whiting & Associates (EWAStock.com)/Andreas von Einsiedel; **120** Elizabeth Whiting & Associates/EWAStock.com; **121** Photozest/Inside/S Anton; **127** IPC Syndication/*Homes & Gardens*/Polly Wreford; **132** IPC Syndication/*Homes & Gardens*/Polly Wreford; **133** Red Cover/Simon McBride; **138** IPC Syndication/*Country Homes & Gardens*/Lizzie Orme; **139** IPC Syndication/*Ideal Home*/Spike Powell; **back cover (right)** Red Cover/Alun Callender.

All other photography © Weldon Owen Inc./Pottery Barn: **50 (bottom right), 118-119, 134-135, 140-141** Melanie Acevedo; **88-91, 94, 97, 101, 107** Hotze Eisma; **61, 82 (left)** Jim Franco; **6, 40-41, 43, 50 (top right), 54-57, 142-143, back cover (left)** Mark Lund; **5, 14-15, 18, 50 (left), 51-53, 67 (left), 80, 82 (right), 85 (bottom), 96 (bottom), 100 (right), 108-109, 122-124, 128-131, 136-137** Stefano Massei; **62, 66, 67 (right), 76-77, 81, 84** David Matheson; **24-25, 35, 48-49, 104, 125** Prue Ruscoe; **1, 11, 20-21, 27-28, 36** Alan Williams.

Special thanks to photography researchers Nadine Bazar and Sarah Airey.